Whacky And Whimsical Poetry

A Poetry Collection

Peps Pinnicle

Table of Contents

The Great Golden Cook-Off!..1

Rome-Ant And Ant-Iet...4

The Bixby Bear Who Outsmarted The Hunters 5

The Fool And The Flying Ship 10

The Worm And The Bird 13

The Scarecrow And The Troll..16

Beauty And The Beep 20

The Man And The Genie 22

The Fish In The Time Loop 25

The Mighty Grizzlehorn 28

The Boy Who Couldn't Stop Bouncing..30

The Bungle-Bee's Dilemma 32

Buster The Breeze Bender 34

The Great Hunt Of Hoo-Ha Hill 37

The Wiggly Wonk's Journey 41

The Perilous Strife Of Professor Poof 43

The FizzleFlop Tree 45

Hansel And Gretel's Sugary Test..47

The Last Leaf...50

How To Train Your Doodlebeast 52

Fleeting Reflections 55

The Twelve Labours Of Hercules 57

The Juggler's Plight 61

Alice In Wacky Land 65

Alice Through The Silly Glass 68

A FairyTale Mixup 71

Why The Vulture Lost It's Feathers..74

How Elephant Got His Trunk...78

Why Lion Roars So Loud 82

How Chameleon Got His Colors 85

About The Author...90

The Great Golden Cook-Off!

PEPS PINNICLE

Come one, come all, to the cook-off today!
Where chefs of all kinds will compete and display,
Their zaniest dishes, their quirkiest flair,
For the grand Golden Spatula waiting up there!

First up was old Tim, who made Mushroomy Stew,
But his mushrooms were purple and smelled like shampoo!
They bubbled and wiggled, they jiggled like jelly,
And somehow they danced when they slipped to your belly!

Then Sally McSplice made her Spaghetti Clouds,
They floated like fluff, and they drew in the crowds!
One bite sent you soaring high up to the moon,
To drift like a balloon 'til you came down too soon.

Next came Chef Ralph with his Pickle Surprise,
A pie made of pickles and ten kinds of fries!
But wait—what's that smell? Is it sugar or cheese?
No! It's topped with whipped cream and a hint of old peas.

Don't forget Dapper Dan and his Crunchy Fish Cake,
Made with glittering goldfish and gooey pancake!
He served it with syrup that sparkled bright blue,
The judges just blinked—no one knew what to do!

And let's not ignore quirky Jilly Van Pop,
Her soup was just popcorn that would never stop!
It popped and it crackled and flew through the air,
Landing on judges and in *everyone's* hair!

But the winner that day was a chef named Louise,

WHACKY AND WHIMSICAL POETRY

Who made Ice Cream Lasagna with donuts and peas!
The layers were wild—noodles of fudge,
The judges all drooled, and they just couldn't budge!

With a cheer and a grin, Louise won the spatula,
And everyone danced—it was quite spectacular!
So come next year to this kooky display,
Where chefs cook up dishes in the wildest way!

Rome-Ant And Ant-Iet

WHACKY AND WHIMSICAL POETRY

In a far-away land, 'neath a grand garden tree,
Lived two ant colonies, as mad as can be.
The Reds and the Blacks—oh, how they would fight!
From morning to evening, from day until night.

But deep in the soil, where no one could see,
Two ants fell in love, as it wasn't meant to be!
One was young Rome-ant, a brave little Red,
And sweet Ant-iet, with a heart full of dread.

For Ant-iet's family, all strong and all Black,
Would never allow such a love to unpack.
And Rome-ant's family, oh, what a mess!
They'd crush any Black ant who dared to confess!

One day, at a picnic, 'neath the great rose,
Rome-ant and Ant-iet met right under your nose.
With crumbs all around them, they made quite a pact—
To love one another, no matter their act!

They snuck into tunnels, they whispered by leaves,
They danced on small petals, while hiding from thieves.
But soon came the clash of the colonies fierce,
And poor Ant-iet's heart felt like it would pierce.

Rome-ant cried out, "Oh, why must we fight?
We could share all the crumbs, and all would be right!"
But the ants wouldn't hear it, too stubborn, too mean,
They just wanted war for the garden they'd seen.

So Rome-ant and Ant-iet, with love in their heart,

PEPS PINNICLE

Decided one night that they simply must part.
But not from each other—from the whole crazy lot,
They'd run off together, no matter the plot!

They packed up their leaf, with bits of croissant,
And scurried away to a land far beyond.
Where Reds and Blacks danced, where the sun always set,
And no one would care if they'd ever once met.

Now ants in the garden still argue, it's true,
But Rome-ant and Ant-iet, they bid them adieu!
So if you should see two ants, happy and free,
Just know love can blossom, even under a tree!

The Bixby Bear Who Outsmarted The Hunters

PEPS PINNICLE

In the heart of the woods, near a tree that was tall,
Lived a bear who was clever, the sharpest of all.
His name was old Bixby, and oh, what a brain!
He'd outwit a hunter again and again.

The hunters would gather with traps and with nets,
With rifles and arrows and sneaky mindsets.
But Bixby would grin, with a twinkle and gleam,
He had tricks up his fur, he'd destroy every scheme!

One day in the meadow, the hunters did creep,
With plans to catch Bixby while he was asleep.
But Bixby, oh Bixby, he wasn't that slow,
He rigged up a hammock and stuffed it with snow!

The hunters cried, "Ha! Now we've caught that big brute!"
But they pounced on a snow pile—oh, wasn't that cute?
From the bushes nearby, Bixby chuckled with glee,
And scampered away as they all yelled, "Oh, flee!"

Another time, hunters came armed to the teeth,
With snares and big nets all hiding beneath.
But Bixby knew better, and dug a deep pit,
Then covered it lightly, his best little trick!

The hunters came marching, all proud as could be,
But suddenly fell into Bixby's trap—wee!
They tumbled and stumbled, all tangled in rope,
While Bixby sat high, just chomping his soap.

They tried again later, with pots full of honey,

Thinking the bear would find that quite funny.
But Bixby knew well, oh, he wouldn't be had,
He traded the pots with a porcupine lad!

The Fool And The Flying Ship

The Fool and the Flying Ship

Art By Leo

Peps Pinnicle

WHACKY AND WHIMSICAL POETRY

In a village far off, where the winds softly blow,
Lived a Fool, young and simple, with nothing to show.
His brothers were clever, his parents were proud,
But the Fool was forgotten, lost in the crowd.

One day, the Tsar, with a booming command,
Said, "Bring me a flying ship, as grand as the land!
Whoever can do it shall marry my kin,
The princess herself—let the quest now begin!"

The Fool heard the words, though they seemed quite absurd,
Yet he thought, "Why not try? Perhaps I'll be heard."
With bread from his mother and courage in tow,
He set off on a journey, not knowing where to go.

Through forests and fields, he wandered alone,
Till he met an old man with a heart like stone.
The man asked for bread, and the Fool gave a slice,
For kindness came easy, he didn't think twice.

The old man then smiled, his face warm and bright,
He said, "Fool, my dear, you've done what is right.
For your simple heart and the kindness you give,
I'll grant you a gift—something wondrous to live!"

With a wave of his hand, the old man did shape
A ship made of wood, that rose and escaped.
A flying ship! It sailed in the sky,
And the Fool of the World watched it soar high!

He climbed aboard, and as he flew,

PEPS PINNICLE

He met strange folk with powers too.
A man who could drink the river dry,
A runner so fast he'd vanish by.
A marksman with arrows that never would miss,
A listener who heard every whisper and hiss.

Together they travelled, the Fool and his crew,
To the Tsar's grand palace, where the winds blew.
The Tsar saw the ship, floating high in the air,
But set them strange tasks, tricky and rare.

"Drain the lake!" cried the Tsar, with a mischievous grin.
But the drinker was ready, and emptied it thin.
"Fetch me my daughter's ring from the sea!"
The runner dashed off, as quick as could be.

"Shoot that bird, far off in the sky!"
The marksman took aim, and watched it die.
And the listener, oh, with his sharpest ear,
He knew when danger was coming near.

At last, the Tsar sighed, for his tests had all failed,
The Fool and his friends had easily prevailed.
So the Fool married the princess, with joy in his heart,
And the ship kept flying, a wondrous art.

Though he started as simple, with nothing but bread,
The Fool of the World rose high overhead.
For kindness and friends can carry you far,
Even to places as high as the Tsar.

The Worm And The Bird

PEPS PINNICLE

There once was a worm, both clever and sly,
Who wriggled and wriggled 'neath a bright blue sky.
His name was Squirm, and he knew from the start,
That brains, not brawn, would set him apart.

One fine day, a bird swooped low,
Her beak sharp and ready, her hunger aglow.
She spotted poor Squirm and thought with glee,
"A wriggly worm is just right for me!"

But Squirm wasn't scared, no, not in the least,
Though he faced becoming a feathered feast.
He thought for a moment, then gave a small grin,
For Squirm had a plan to surely win.

"Dear Bird," he called, with a flick of his tail,
"I know you're hungry, and I look quite frail,
But why settle for one worm, when there's more to eat?
I know a place with a grander treat!"

The bird tilted her head and gave it some thought,
What could be better than the worm she had caught?
But curiosity won, and her hunger grew strong—
She decided to follow Squirm right along.

"Just follow me!" Squirm said with delight,
"I'll lead you to something so tasty, just right!"
Through the garden and past a big leafy tree,
He led the bird closer to what it could be.

They came to a pond, murky and deep,

With ripples that danced and shadows that creep.
"Look!" said Squirm, pointing down with his tail,
"A mountain of worms! More than you'd ever inhale!"

The bird peered over, her beady eyes wide,
As bubbles rose up from the water's dark tide.
She stretched out her neck, leaning too far,
When suddenly—**SPLASH**—there came a bizarre!

A catfish leaped up, fast as a shot,
Its mouth opened wide, and with one great "GLOP!"
It snapped at the bird, with a quick, giant bite,
And down she went—gone, out of sight!

Squirm wiggled with glee, safe and sound,
As the pond grew still, not a peep nor a sound.
He chuckled to himself, so proud of his trick,
For he knew he was one smart, quick-witted stick.

And so Squirm squirmed on, as happy as can be,
Outsmarting the bird, with great victory.
For in the garden, both sly and wise,
It's not always the biggest who wins the prize!

The Scarecrow And The Troll

WHACKY AND WHIMSICAL POETRY

In a field full of corn, there stood tall and proud,
A scarecrow named Crowley, who boasted out loud:
"I'm the best scarecrow you'll ever see,
No crow dare to nibble a kernel near me!"

But one dark night, a shadow did creep,
A troll named Grizzle, from the forest deep.
He growled and he grumbled with a terrible scowl,
For his shiny treasures were gone, with a foul!

"The crows have taken my glittering gold,
And it's *your* fault, scarecrow—so brazen, so bold!"
Crowley just chuckled, "Oh Grizzle, dear friend,
The crows love me, they don't need to offend!"

Grizzle leaned in, his eyes full of might,
"If you're so smart, then riddle me right!
Three questions I'll ask, answer true if you dare,
Or I'll turn you to feathers and throw you in the air!"

Crowley laughed, waving a hand in dismissal,
"I'm ready, old troll, your riddles are dismal!"
So the troll began, with a sneaky grin,
A test for the scarecrow too lazy to win.

First Riddle:
"What's light as a feather but can't be held tight,
It whispers through trees, in the dead of night?"

Crowley rolled his eyes, with a snort of disdain,
"That's easy, dear Grizzle, it's nothing but rain!"

But the troll just cackled, "Ha! Wrong, you fool!
It's the *wind* that whispers, you arrogant tool!"

Crowley frowned but still stood tall,
"I'll get the next one, just try and make me fall!"

Second Riddle:
"What has no legs, but runs like the wind,
And cuts through mountains, with waters that bend?"

Crowley yawned, bored with the troll's petty game,
"Why, that's clearly a horse—this is getting so lame!"
Grizzle grinned wide and shook his head slow,
"No, it's a *river* that runs, how little you know!"

Crowley was rattled, but he stayed on his toes,
"I'll ace the next one, just watch how it goes!"

Third Riddle:
"What's shiny and gold, but cannot be sold,
It rises each day, in a sky that's bold?"

Crowley smirked, "A treasure, no doubt,
That's the gold in your cave, rolling about!"
Grizzle howled with laughter, his face all aglow,
"You foolish scarecrow, it's the *sun*, don't you know?"

And with that last laugh, Grizzle raised his hand,
Magic swirling from his fingers like sand.
Crowley gasped as he felt himself shrink,
Feathers sprouted out faster than he could think!

With a flash and a crash, Crowley shrank in surprise,
Feathers fluttered out, and wings took the prize!
"Caw-caw!" he screeched, flapping high in dismay,
The arrogant scarecrow was a crow, now to stay.

Grizzle chuckled, his shiny teeth aglow,
"That's what you get for being so slow.
You had one job, and now you're done,
Crows can't scare crows—you've just begun!"

So off flew Crowley, with feathers of black,
No longer proud, with no chance to go back.
He learned too late, with a squawk and a cry,
That laziness leads to a feathered goodbye!

Beauty And The Beep

WHACKY AND WHIMSICAL POETRY

In a land far away, where the trees chirp and peep,
Lived a clunky ol' robot, they called him the Beep!
With gears that went whirr and bolts that went thunk,
He wasn't so scary—just rusty and clunk.

He lived in a tower, all lonely and grim,
For who would want tea with a robot so dim?
His circuits were fried, his smile was a glitch,
But deep in his core, he just had an itch—

An itch to be loved, to be seen as more,
Than a clattering, clanking, mechanical bore!
Then along came Hanna, with her books and her flair,
She wasn't afraid of the grease in his hair!

"Hello there!" she said, "What's all the fuss?
You don't scare me, Beep, you just need a tune-up!"
She polished his buttons, she tightened a screw,
And little by little, their friendship just grew.

They danced 'round the tower, as gears clicked and beeped,
And soon Beep found love—he no longer just creeped!
For it wasn't his circuits, his bolts, or his sheen,
That made him a friend—it's the heart in between.

So remember, dear reader, as you hum through the day,
Even a robot can love, in their own special way.
For beauty's not found in the rust or the crease,
But in kindness and care—from the Beep to the "Beast!"

The Man And The Genie

WHACKY AND WHIMSICAL POETRY

Once in a desert, all dusty and dry,
A man found a lamp with a glimmering eye.
He gave it a rub, and with puff and a spin,
Out came a genie, with a sly little grin!

"Oh, master, oh master," the genie did shout,
"I'll grant you three wishes, there's no need to doubt!
Ask anything—riches or kingdoms so grand,
I'm here to obey your every command!"

The man scratched his chin and thought for a bit,
He knew in his heart that the genie was slick.
Genies, you see, have their tricks up their sleeves,
But the man had a plan, something no one believes!

"First wish!" said the man with a glint in his eye,
"I wish for some pie—oh, a slice that's sky high!"
The genie looked puzzled but made it appear,
A pie so delicious, it brought out a cheer.

"For my second wish, oh genie so wise,
I wish for a hat that can shrink or can rise.
Big when it's raining, and small when it's clear,
A hat that fits perfectly, year after year!"

The genie was baffled but granted it still,
A hat that could stretch or could shrink at will.
He thought, "This is easy, this man's not too smart,
His last wish will be dull—and I'll soon depart!"

But the man wasn't finished; he grinned ear to ear,

PEPS PINNICLE

"Now genie, for my last wish, listen real clear.
I wish that the wishes you granted so free,
Would stick with you, too—so you'll *answer to me!*"

The genie blinked twice, his face turned pale,
For the trick in the wish was beyond the usual tale.
The pie and the hat, they seemed silly and light,
But now *he* was stuck with them, morning and night!

He'd carry that pie wherever he went,
And wear that strange hat—what a wish the man spent!
The genie looked down, with a pie in one hand,
And a hat that kept shrinking, just like the man planned!

"Oh, what have you done?" the genie did cry,
"Now I'm stuck with this nonsense till the day I die!"
The man laughed aloud, "Oh genie, you see,
You may grant wishes, but you're not tricking me!"

So off walked the man, all clever and spry,
While the genie stood there with his pie and hat in the sky.
For sometimes a wish, when twisted just right,
Can fool even the smartest of genies in sight!

So remember this tale, and the clever last twist,
Sometimes it's the simple things that are hard to resist.
For when facing a genie, make sure you're prepared,
A wish can be powerful, if wisely declared!

The Fish In The Time Loop

PEPS PINNICLE

In a pond by the shore, in a world quite absurd,
Lived a fish named Flip, who felt rather disturbed.
He swam round in circles, not once but again,
For poor little Flip was caught in time's spin!

"I swim, I stop, I swim some more,
But each time I finish, I'm back at the shore!"
He flipped and he flopped, his fins in a tizzy,
This loop, oh this loop, was making him dizzy!

He'd leap to the sky with a splash and a swoop,
Only to find he'd returned to his loop!
"The same splash, the same swoosh, the same bubbles of blue,
No matter what I do, it just starts anew!"

"I've tried swimming backwards, I've tried swimming fast,
But no matter the speed, I just loop back at last!"
The frogs on the bank all croaked with a grin,
"You're looping, dear Flip, from the outside and in!"

With a huff and a puff, he swirled in the muck,
But no matter his effort, poor Flip was still stuck.
Each day felt the same, like a tale told twice,
Repeating and spinning, no change, no spice!

But then Flip had a thought, as he looped once again,
"If I'm stuck in a loop, why fight and complain?
What if I enjoy this strange, loopy ride,
And make the best of this watery tide?"

So he flipped with a chuckle, and swirled with delight,

Each loop felt new as he twisted in flight.
The loop wasn't bad, it was just how he swam,
And now Flip, the fish, was a loop-loving clam!

27

The Mighty Grizzlehorn

Up on the peak of Mount Flimsy-Flim-Florn,
Lived a creature of legend, the great Grizzlehorn.
He'd thunder and roar from his cave made of ice,
He'd challenge all comers (but only once or twice).

His horns were so long, his teeth were so bright,
That the whole world below trembled in fright.
But deep down inside, where no one could see,
The Grizzlehorn sighed—he just wanted to flee.

He roared and he stomped, but it wasn't much fun,
For the Grizzlehorn felt like his roaring was done.
He looked to the valley, with a tear in his eye,
And thought, "Is it worth it, this life up so high?"

The Grizzlehorn slumped, with a sorrowful moan,
He looked up to the stars, feeling empty and alone.
And though no one heard him, his roar became small,
Until it was nothing. No sound left at all.

The Boy Who Couldn't Stop Bouncing

WHACKY AND WHIMSICAL POETRY

Young Billy McBounce was a boy on the run,
He bounced and he bounced, just for fun in the sun!
He leaped over fences, he bounced over trees,
He hopped past the rivers and jumped past the seas!

He couldn't sit still, not a minute, not one,
For bouncing and jumping was Billy's own fun.
His feet never stopped, his legs were a blur,
He bounced through the meadows, his heart all a-whirr.

But one fateful day, as he soared through the sky,
Billy bounced high—far too high, oh my!
He jumped through the clouds, and he bounced to the moon,
But that was the moment he realized too soon...

That what goes up high must come down, yes indeed,
But Billy, dear Billy, paid no mind to the speed.
And as he came falling, with no place to land,
He wished he'd just walked—oh, if only he'd planned.

Now Billy's still bouncing, in the great starry void,
No Earth beneath him, just nothing—destroyed.
For sometimes too much fun can lead you astray,
And leave you quite lost, in the darkest of day.

The Bungle-Bee's Dilemma

WHACKY AND WHIMSICAL POETRY

In the land of Wuzwinkles, by the Jibble-Jo tree,
Lived a fuzzy, round creature called Bungle-Bee.
With wings made of buttons and legs made of strings,
He loved to buzz high, over marvelous things.

But one sunny morning, with a bumble and breeze,
Bungle-Bee stopped by the Prickledown Seas.
"I can't fly today!" Bungle cried with a tear,
"My wings have grown heavy; my buzzing's unclear!"

He tried and he tried, with a *buzz* and a *whirr,*
But his wings only flopped, not a flicker nor blur.
"Oh no!" he declared, "What's happened to me?
I must find the answer! I must find the key!"

He waddled to Doctor Floop's very tall spire,
Where bubbles were floating and wires spun higher.
"Doctor, dear Doctor, I can't seem to fly!
My wings won't go up; I don't know why!"

The Doctor just chuckled and adjusted his specs,
"Your wings are too full! They're a bit of a wreck.
You've gathered too much of the dust from the trees,
The pollen and fluff from the Jibble-Jo breeze!"

With a laugh and a brush, and a spin like a top,
The Doctor cleaned Bungle, from bottom to mop!
Now light as a feather, with wings clear and bright,
Bungle-Bee soared up into the light!

Buster The Breeze Bender

WHACKY AND WHIMSICAL POETRY

In a world full of elements—four, not just three,
Lived Bluster, the bender of wind and of glee.
He could twirl up a gust with a flick of his hand,
And make leaves do the tango all over the land.

The Fire Folks flickered with sparks from their toes,
And the Water Clan splashed with their elegant flows.
The Earth Tribe, they rumbled with rocks in the air,
But Bluster just floated without any care.

One day came a storm, big and burly and loud,
With clouds full of thunder that rumbled and plowed.
"Oh no!" cried the people, "It's far worse than rain,
We need a strong bender to battle this bane!"

Bluster flew in with a whoosh and a whirl,
His scarf spinning wildly, his hair in a curl.
"I'll puff and I'll huff, I'll calm this wild storm,
I'll bend it with breezes, smooth, light, and warm!"

He twirled up a cyclone, but not with much care,
It wobbled and wiggled and jumbled the air.
Then the storm got much bigger, a wild, crazy sight,
Bluster had made it a whirlwind of fright!

"Oh dear!" cried the people, "Our bender's too bold,
His winds have gone wild, we're out of control!"
But Bluster just smiled, gave a wink and a nod,
"I'll bend it again with a trick that's quite odd!"

He blew a soft breeze, gentle and low,

And the storm started shrinking, as slow as it'd grow.
The lightning dissolved into sparkles of blue,
And the thunder just chuckled, then faded from view.

The people all cheered as the sky became clear,
And Bluster, the Breeze-Bender, twirled in the air.
"I've learned," he declared, with his feet off the ground,
"That gentle's the way when the storms come around."

So Bluster, our hero, both clever and kind,
Taught everyone balance—of heart and of mind.
For the best benders know, in the wildest weather,
It's not just raw power—it's bringing things *together*

The Great Hunt Of Hoo-Ha Hill

PEPS PINNICLE

In the land of Tumble, on Hoo-Ha Hill,
There existed a great contest of skill and will.
The hunters all gathered with bows, nets, and spears,
To see who could claim the prize of the year.

Mayor McDuffle stood tall on a stump,
With a booming big voice and a gentleman's hump.
He waved to the crowd and called them all near,
"The Great Hunt is starting! Now lend me your ear!"

"The rules are quite simple, you must hunt with care,
But not for just rabbits, or foxes, or hares.
The prize of the day is the Sneaky-Wonk beast,
A creature that's known for dodging our feasts!"

"It's slipperier than fish, and quicker than wind,
It hides in the shadows, it slips through our rings!
But whoever can catch this elusive old friend,
Will win the grand trophy—right here at the end!"

The hunters all cheered and sharpened their blades,
With their nets in their hands and their traps in the shade.
Off they all dashed, through valleys and trees,
As the wind whistled wild through the cool autumn breeze.

First came young Jilly, with her trusty old slingshot,
But her aim was too wobbly, the Sneaky-Wonk she caught not.
She tumbled and bumbled through bushes and thorns,
While the beast slipped away with a bounce and a scorn.

Next came old Grizzle, with a net made of steel,

"I'll catch that sly Wonky! It's a sure deal!"
But he stumbled and tripped on a rock by the stream,
And the Sneaky-Wonk vanished, as quick as a dream.

Then brave Hunter Blue, with his bow drawn so tight,
Thought he'd surely catch it, it was well in his sight.
But the Sneaky-Wonk darted, just as fast as can be,
And poor Hunter Blue was left stuck in a tree!

The sun started sinking, the day nearly done,
But no hunter had caught that slippery one.
They scratched their heads, their brows full of sweat,
For that Sneaky-Wonk just 0wasn't a prize they could get.

But then out from the woods came little Pip Monique,
The smallest of hunters, with shoes that would squeak.
No traps in her hand, no bow and no dart,
Just a basket of berries and a kind, gentle heart.

She tiptoed through meadows and softly did hum,
And there in the bushes, did that Sneaky-Wonk come!
It sniffed at her basket, with eyes big and wide,
And Pip, without fear, simply knelt by its side.

"Here you go, Wonky, some berries to eat,
No need for a chase, no need for defeat."
The Sneaky-Wonk smiled, took a bite, then two,
And followed young Pip, as though it just knew.

Back to the crowd, they strolled side by side,
With Pip at the front, and the Wonky with pride.

PEPS PINNICLE

The hunters all gasped, their jaws open wide,
For Pip had won, without needing to hide!

Mayor McDuffle raised Pip's hand with glee,
"Pip Monique has won, quite marvellously!
No chasing or fighting, no traps and no tricks,
Just kindness, berries and sugary sticks"

The Wiggly Wonk's Journey

PEPS PINNICLE

The Wiggly-Wonk set off on a quest,
To climb the great mountain, the land's biggest test.
With a bag full of dreams and a heart full of cheer,
He wobbled and wiggled with nothing to fear.

The paths twisted wildly, the winds howled loud,
But the Wiggly-Wonk pushed through every dark cloud.
He laughed at the boulders, he skipped over streams,
His eyes fixed on the top, where gleamed all his dreams.

But when he arrived, oh, what a surprise,
The peak was so empty, no prize met his eyes.
The mountain was silent, the journey was done,
And the Wiggly-Wonk's heart, it no longer felt fun.

For sometimes the climb, though it brings you up high,
Can leave you alone with just an empty sky.
And the dreams that once sparkled, so distant and bright,
Can feel far too heavy when you reach that great height.

The Perilous Strife Of Professor Poof

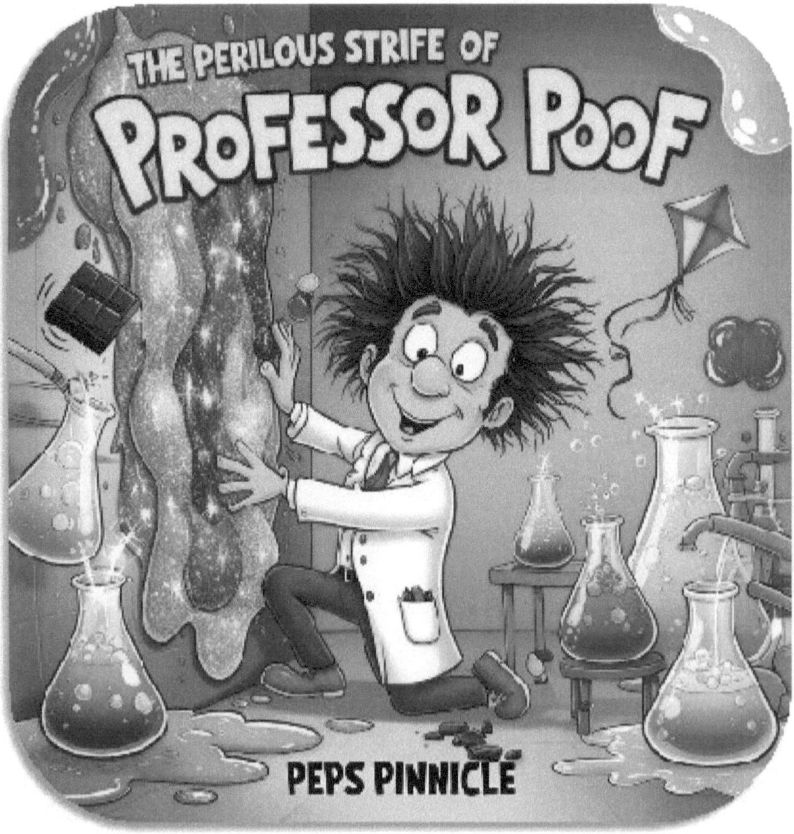

PEPS PINNICLE

Professor Poof had a marvellous brain,
It bubbled with wonders that drove him insane!
He'd think up inventions both silly and bright,
Like a chocolate-powered kite that could soar out of sight.

But one day, oh dear, while mixing a brew,
He added green glitter, and it stuck like glue!
It bubbled and fizzed and grew much too tall,
And soon enough, Poof was stuck to the wall.

He scrambled and wiggled, he tugged and he clanked,
But the glittery goo just wouldn't be yanked!
Then with a loud sneeze—KA-BOOM—it was gone,
And Poof stood there laughing, right out on the lawn.

The FizzleFlop Tree

PEPS PINNICLE

In a land far away where the sky's always green,
And the critters wear hats made of tangerine sheen,
There grows a tall tree, oh, as odd as can be,
They call it the twisty, tall Fizzleflop Tree!

Its branches curl 'round like a candy cane hook,
With marshmallow leaves and a bubblegum look,
Its fruit, when it drops, doesn't splat—it goes pop!
And bounces back up like a spring-loaded top.

Now, under this tree lives a fellow named Wheeze,
With shoes made of sparkles and pants up to his knees.
He sings silly songs about marmalade pie,
And dances in circles with birds that can fly!

One day, as he danced with a bounce and a twirl,
A strange little creature popped out with a whirl.
Its nose was a trumpet, its tail a balloon,
It whistled and whooped to a topsy-tune!

"I'm a Snicker-Snuck from the land of Kazoo,
Where clouds are all purple, and rivers are blue!
I've come here to see what the Fizzleflop grows,
I've heard there are wonders, like liquorice crows!"

Wheeze laughed and he spun, with a clatter and clap,
And handed the Snuck a sweet taffy-wrapped sap.
"It's true," Wheeze exclaimed, "but be careful, my friend,
Once you start in this land, the fun never ends!"

Hansel And Gretel's Sugary Test

PEPS PINNICLE

Hansel and Gretel, two children so bright,
Set off through the woods in the dim, fading light.
With crumbs on the ground to mark their way back,
But oh no! The birds ate their breadcrumb track!

They wandered and wandered, all lost and alone,
Till deep in the forest, a house made of stone!
But wait—it's not stone, it's something much sweeter—
The walls made of candy, from roof down to meter!

"Oh, Hansel, oh Gretel," the house seemed to say,
"Come closer, come closer, and munch right away!"
With candy so tasty, and cookies galore,
How could they resist? They knocked on the door!

Out came the witch, with a cackle and grin,
"Oh, my dear children, please, do come in!
I've sweets, I've treats, for you to devour,
Just sit, little dears, and stay for an hour."

But sneaky old Hansel, he smelled something foul,
For the witch's kind face hid a plan so vile.
She locked him in cages, and fed him with bread,
"Grow plump!" she cackled, "for soon you'll be fed!"

But clever young Gretel had plans of her own,
She played the good girl, never once did she moan.
She waited and watched, till the time was just right,
Then pushed the old witch into the oven, out of sight!

The house of sweet candy soon melted away,

And Hansel was free! Oh, what a day!
Together they left, with their hearts full of cheer,
Homeward they marched, for their path was now clear.

So Hansel and Gretel, so brave and so clever,
Showed that with courage, you can win out forever!

The Last Leaf

WHACKY AND WHIMSICAL POETRY

On a tree full of green, with leaves all aglow,
There sat one last leaf, too stubborn to go.
The others had left, swept away by the breeze,
They'd flown from the branches and danced through the trees.

But this one remained, clinging tight to its twig,
While winter approached and the cold grew quite big.
It shivered each day as the winds howled near,
But it held on with hope, through every fear.

Then one chilly night, with a soft little sound,
That brave final leaf fluttered down to the ground.
It twirled in the air, its journey complete,
And the tree stood bare, silent and sweet.

How To Train Your Doodlebeast

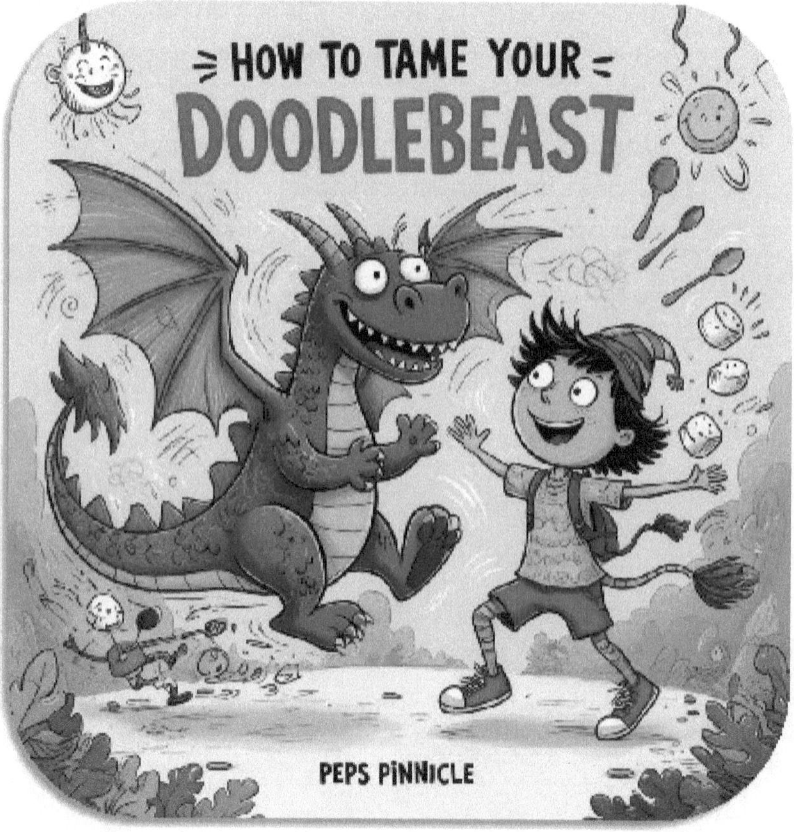

WHACKY AND WHIMSICAL POETRY

Have you ever seen creatures with wings all askew?
With scales of bright purple and tails painted blue?
They zip through the skies with a roar and a feast—
Why, you must have encountered a wild Doodlebeast!

Now Doodlebeasts, mind you, are quite hard to tame,
They're stubborn and silly, and none are the same.
They doodle in doodles, they scribble in flight,
And some even snore in the middle of night!

But fear not, young friend, for taming's a trick—
It's all in the way that you think really quick!
Forget all the books and the nets that they bring,
You can't catch a Doodle with a regular thing.

You'll need something odd and something neat—
Like tickling its belly with socks on your feet!
Or balancing spoons on the tip of your nose,
That's how you'll impress them, that's how it goes!

For a Doodlebeast loves the peculiar and wild,
They bond with the ones who are weird as a child.
If you juggle marshmallows or dance in a sock,
A Doodlebeast giggles—oh, they'll be in shock!

Once they are laughing, it's time for step two,
You'll hop on its back and shout out, "YAHOO!"
But hold on quite tight, for they zigzag and dart,
Doodlebeasts, you see, are not for the faint heart.

They'll loop-de-loop upward, then dive to the ground,

PEPS PINNICLE

You'll feel like you're stuck on a merry-go-round!
But once they calm down and their sillies are through,
They'll snuggle up close and be loyal to you.

Now you've tamed your Doodle, hooray and hooroo!
But remember, my friend, what you've got to do:
Keep them well-fed on jellybean pies,
And tell them tall stories that stretch to the skies!

For Doodlebeasts thrive on laughter and play,
They don't like to fight or to frighten away.
So grab your best hat, wear mismatched socks,
And teach your Doodle some new fancy tricks and talks!

So there you have it, the taming's complete,
With giggles and games, you've mastered the feat!
Now off you both fly, with a flap and a soar,
The Doodlebeast's yours—forevermore!

Fleeting Reflections

PEPS PINNICLE

Oh, I look to the sky with a curious gaze,
When the world is all quiet, in a sleepy haze.
What's life like ahead, when my paths are all worn?
When the sun sets its glow and the day greets the morn?

Of all the grand tales that have danced in my head,
And all the sweet songs that have fluttered and fled,
Nothing feels quite as heavy, oh dear, oh my,
As the thought of a life that must say its goodbye.

The sky can be blue, too blue, oh so bright!
Like a paint splatter gone wild in the soft morning light.
It's vibrant and cheery, but sometimes a mess,
Like a cobbler's old shoe in a terrible dress!

But I wish for the stars to be brighter, hooray!
When I gaze at the night, in a dreamy ballet.
I want them to twinkle, to sparkle and glow,
Not just little dots with a faint, muted show!

Yet, through all my adventures and wishes galore,
There's one little hope that I hold to my core:
I wish that my mirror, so shiny and bright,
Would show me the truth on the darkest of nights.

But what if one day, that mirror should crack?
Reflecting a shadow, a figure turned black.
For in all of my wandering, in dreams that I weave,
The saddest of endings is to never believe.

The Twelve Labours Of Hercules

PEPS PINNICLE

Hercules, Hercules, mighty and strong,
Faced tasks so daring, some dreadfully long.
Twelve were the labours he had to complete,
Let's hop on the journey and follow his feet!

First was the lion, all covered in gold,
Its hide was too tough for hands to take hold.
But Hercules caught it, with strength and with flair,
He wrestled that lion right out of its lair!

Then came the hydra, with heads full of fright,
Each time one was chopped, two more would ignite.
But clever Herc burned where each head had once been,
And soon the hydra was no more to be seen.

Next, he chased down the hind, oh so fleet,
With hooves like a whisper, so light on its feet.
For a whole year he chased that deer through the wood,
Till finally, gently, he captured it good!

The boar on the mountain was next to defeat,
A pig so enormous, it stomped with great heat.
Through snow and through wind, he gave it no slack,
And dragged it down screaming right over his back!

The stables of Augeas, so filthy, so wide,
Were filled with manure up to the side.
But Hercules thought, "I know what to do!"
He redirected rivers and flushed it right through.

The birds at the lake, with wings sharp as steel,

WHACKY AND WHIMSICAL POETRY

Flew over the waters with dangerous zeal.
But Herc clanged his shield, loud as a roar,
And scared them all off, so they troubled no more.

The bull from Crete, snorting fire from its nose,
Trampled through towns and flattened the rows.
But Hercules grabbed it, calm and serene,
And led it away, like it'd never been mean.

Next came the horses of Diomedes, wild,
With terrible hunger and ways most defiled.
Herc fed them their master—oh, what a shock!—
And soon those mean horses were tame as a rock.

To steal Hippolyta's belt was the plan,
From the warrior queen and her Amazon clan.
But the gods stirred up trouble; a battle ensued!
Herc took that belt in the middle of the feud.

The cattle of Geryon, guarded by three,
With three-headed Geryon as fierce as could be.
But Herc struck him down with a swing of his hand,
And gathered the cows from that faraway land.

Now, for the apples of gold from the trees,
Guarded by dragons that hissed in the breeze.
But Atlas, the titan, helped Herc with his plea,
And lifted the world while Herc gathered all three.

The last was the hardest, to fetch from the dead,
The hound of the underworld, Cerberus, dread.

PEPS PINNICLE

But with courage and strength that could never retire,
Herc led the dog out without a single fire.

Twelve were the labors, and oh, what a tale!
Through monsters, through rivers, through dragons and gale.
Hercules triumphed, as heroes should do,
And now his adventures are shared here with you!

The Juggler's Plight

PEPS PINNICLE

There once was a man from the town of Tally Tack,
Who'd juggle and fumble, and act quite off track.
He'd kick and he'd holler, he'd twirl and he'd spit,
Till the townsfolk all said, "We've had enough of it!"

"Get out!" they all shouted, "We can't take your flair!"
But the man only blinked, wide-eyed and sincere.
"I'm sorry!" he said, "But it's just how I be,
I juggle, I juggle, it's part of being me!"

So they gathered their junk: pots, pans, and big clocks,
Hats, gloves, and old shoes, cement blocks, and socks!
"Let's throw it all at him!" they said with a cheer,
"We'll drive him out, so he'll disappear!"

The next day he came, with a twitch and a shake,
"Why is it so quiet? Something feels fake..."
No ducks, no bugs, not a soul to be found,
Till suddenly doors burst open all around!

Out came apples, frozen, hard as a rock,
Books, chairs, dogs, cats—even old man MayBerry's socks!
They flung every item they could toss in the air,
And the juggler? He caught them without even a care!

He spun and he twirled, he flipped and he flew,
His hands were so fast, no one quite knew
How kettles and clocks and tyres and shoes
Sailed up to the sky like there was nothing to lose.

"Is this all you've got?" the juggler did scoff,

WHACKY AND WHIMSICAL POETRY

"Keep throwing! Keep tossing! I'll never fall off!"
His hands were like lightning, so nimble, so quick,
He juggled and grinned, and performed every trick.

The people kept throwing, but soon they all stopped—
They'd thrown all they had, the last penny had dropped.
Their houses were empty, the cupboards were bare,
Not a single old trinket was left anywhere.

The juggler stood tall, with his hat still in place,
When suddenly something flew right past his face—
A butterfly, golden, so soft and so light,
It shimmered and sparkled, a magical sight!

He reached for the beauty, all smug with his skill,
But it slipped through his fingers—oh, what a thrill!
And down came the pots, the kettles, the pans,
Down came the plates and the fans and the cans!

CRASH! went the clutter, CLANG! went the junk,
The juggler went down with a big mighty thunk.
He lay in a heap, all battered and bruised,
While the town stood and stared, slightly confused.

But his hat! His blue hat, not a tear or a crack,
It sat there untouched, still on his back.
The man groaned and wheezed, as he lay in a sprawl,
"I guess," he sighed, "I'm not that good after all..."

And with a wink and a grin, though bruised to the core,
He whispered, "Maybe... juggling's not what I'm for."

PEPS PINNICLE

Then he looked to the sky, all wobbly and little,
"I should've, perhaps... learned to play the fiddle?"

64

Alice In Wacky Land

PEPS PINNICLE

In a land that was wibbly and wobbly, too,
Lived a girl named Alice, with a big floppy shoe.
She chased a strange rabbit, all dressed up in style,
With a watch made of chocolate and a mischievous smile.

"Oh dear!" said the rabbit, with a twitch of his ear,
"I'm late for a party—come quick! It's right near!"
So, Alice, quite curious, skipped after the hare,
Through a doorway that led to a world beyond compare.

There were flowers that giggled and trees made of gum,
And a cat with a grin that said, "What's your fun?"
The Cheshire Cat chuckled, his stripes all askew,
"Why not join the Mad Hatter for tea and a stew?"

So they sat at a table where teacups could talk,
And pastries did pirouettes, dancing on the clock.
"Drink this!" said the Hatter, with a wink and a nod,
"It's a brew full of wonders—just give it a prod!"

Alice sipped from her cup, and her eyes opened wide,
As the table turned into a wild, crazy ride!
With hats flying high and a tea storm of glee,
They zoomed through the air, "Oh, this is the key!"

Then came a strange creature, all fuzzy and bright,
With a grin like a crescent and wings that took flight.
"I'm the Snicker-Snack Boodle!" it twirled in the sky,
"Let's play a fine game of catch with a pie!"

They tossed and they rolled with sweet splats of delight,

WHACKY AND WHIMSICAL POETRY

While the flowers cheered on, blooming colors so bright.
But soon the sun started to sink in the day,
And Alice knew it was time to be on her way.

"Goodbye, wibbly world, with your nonsense so grand!
I'll carry your whimsy wherever I stand!"
She skipped back through the doorway, her heart full of cheer,
For in wild, wacky lands, adventure is near!

And though she returned to her life oh-so-plain,
She'd always remember the joy and the rain,
Of a world that was silly, with friends she could find,
In the heart of her dreams, where the wacky unwind!

Alice Through The Silly Glass

WHACKY AND WHIMSICAL POETRY

Alice was bored, as she often would be,
When she spotted a mirror as tall as a tree.
It shimmered and wobbled with a magical glow,
So she stepped right on in—where else could she go?

On the other side, oh, what did she see?
A land made of puzzles and topsy-turvy tea!
There were spoons that could fly, and clocks that could sing,
And a queen who wore pizza for her royal bling-bling!

"This is the land of the Silly Glass Realm,
Where nonsense is king and the wild things helm!"
A dodo in slippers hopped over with flair,
"Let's juggle these oranges! Just toss them in the air!"

Alice giggled and joined in the fun,
As the oranges bounced like the rays of the sun.
Then came a knight riding a wobbly spoon,
Singing, "I'm the Soggy Knight, and I dance with the moon!"

"Oh dear!" thought young Alice, as she twirled in delight,
"This world is so silly, yet wondrously bright!"
She skipped on her way to a chessboard of pies,
Where the Red Queen was juggling cakes with her eyes!

"Off with their frosting!" the Queen shouted loud,
As sprinkles and icing rained down on the crowd.
But instead of a scare, it was all quite a treat,
For the crowd cheered and danced, never missing a beat.

Then Alice met Humpty, not on a wall,

PEPS PINNICLE

But hopping on pogo sticks, bouncing so tall!
"Through the glass, all is strange!" he declared with a grin,
"The rules here are backwards, and that's where you win!"

As the sun started setting, the mirror called back,
"Time to return, Alice! Pack up your snack!"
So she waved to the queen, to the knight, and the cat,
And zipped through the glass like a quick acrobat.

Back in her room, she gave one final glance,
At the mirror that led to her Silly Glass dance.
And though the world outside may seem just the same,
She knew that through mirrors, there's always a game!

For beyond every glass, in each shiny gleam,
There's a world full of wonders, if only you dream.

A FairyTale Mixup

PEPS PINNICLE

Once in a land, not far from here,
Where all tales you've heard are crystal clear,
The stories combined, like milk and tea,
In a land where the endings weren't meant to be!

Cinderella danced in glassy shoes,
While Snow White sang to birds with the blues,
Little Red skipped, her basket in hand,
And Jack climbed high in the beanstalk land.

But what they didn't know, oh dear, oh dear,
Was something strange was brewing near.
The villains had gathered, wicked and sly,
To change these endings—oh my, oh my!

The Big Bad Wolf, with a huff and puff,
Said, "I'm tired of losing—it's just too tough!"
The Queen with her mirror, so cruel and grim,
Said, "Let's rewrite these tales on a villainous whim!"

Maleficent spread her wings so wide,
Said, "Why can't I win? I've certainly tried!"
And the Witch who lured Hansel and Gretel with treats,
Laughed as she plotted her villainous feats.

They hatched a plan, so cunning and sly,
To make the heroes fail—oh, don't ask why!
Cinderella tripped and lost her shoe,
The clock struck twelve, but she never knew.

Snow White took a bite of the apple so red,

But this time, dear reader, she stayed in bed.
Jack met the Giant, but with no clever scheme,
The beans did nothing—no magical dream.

Little Red lost her way in the wood,
And the Wolf, this time, finished his feast as he should.
The Huntsman got lost, the Prince didn't show,
The fairytale heroes just didn't know.

The villains laughed with a mighty cheer,
For now they were winning year after year.
"At last," said the Queen, with a villainous grin,
"Who said the good guys always must win?"

And in this land, mixed up and spun,
The villains had finally all the fun.
So if you read tales and expect the end bright,
Beware, for the villains might rewrite your night!

Why The Vulture Lost It's Feathers

WHACKY AND WHIMSICAL POETRY

Once in the land of Congo Congo so bright,
Where the sun shone golden from morning to night,
There lived a Vulture, proud and so tall,
With feathers like silk, the finest of all!

Her wings were gleaming, her beak was sleek,
And Vulture, oh Vulture, thought she was unique.
She'd fly up so high with a swoosh and a glide,
No one in Congo Congo could match her in pride.

But Vulture, dear Vulture, had a flaw in her heart,
She'd boast and she'd brag, tearing others apart.
When Peacock would dance, with feathers of blue,
Vulture would cackle, "Oh, I'm better than you!"

She mocked little Sparrow for being too small,
Teased clever Parrot for knowing it all.
She'd strut through the jungle, wings wide and unfurled,
"I'm the finest of birds in the whole wide world!"

But one day the wind brought a curious chill,
And Vulture's feathers grew stiff, then still.
A whisper came blowing through the trees so fair,
"Beware, proud Vulture, of the Greedy Snare!"

She laughed at the warning, scoffing aloud,
"I'm Vulture, the best, I'm perfectly proud!"
Yet that very same night, as the moon shone bright,
A twinkle of trouble appeared in the light.

Out from the bushes came Sly Hyena's grin,

PEPS PINNICLE

With a gleam in his eye and a mischievous spin.
"I'll give you a treasure, the greatest of swoons,
If you lend me your feathers, just for a few moons."

Vulture, intrigued, by this gleaming request,
Thought "I'll trade for more sparkle, my feathers will rest.
And once I've got treasure, I'll be even more grand,
The most dazzling Vulture in all of the land!"

She plucked and she plucked, each feather away,
Handing them off to Hyena that day.
But little did Vulture know with each pull,
Her pride was now leaving, her wings no longer full.

Without her fine feathers, she started to shiver,
The cold of the night made her quiver and quiver.
Hyena, he laughed, "Oh, silly bird,
You've traded your beauty for something absurd!"

And when the sun rose, with a gasp and a cry,
Vulture, now bare, couldn't soar through the sky.
Her pride, once mighty, had vanished and gone,
And Vulture was left all alone at the dawn.

From that day forward, she learned what was true—
That kindness and friendship matter more than you knew.
She watches from trees, her feathers now bare,
But her heart has grown humble, she's learned how to care.

So if you meet Vulture, just offer a smile,
For she's wiser now, and she'll stay for a while.

And remember her tale, whenever you find,
That pride without kindness leaves feathers behind.

How Elephant Got His Trunk

WHACKY AND WHIMSICAL POETRY

In the jungles of Congo Congo, so wide and so grand,
Lived an Elephant, proud, with a nose rather bland.
It was short and quite stubby, not useful at all,
For reaching tall branches or catching a ball.

Elephant grumbled, "Oh, what a shame,
My nose is too short! It's such a bad game!"
He'd watch Giraffe with her neck stretched so high,
And the Monkeys who swung with a whoop and a cry.

"Why can't I reach like they do with ease?
I just want to grab all the fruits from the trees!"
But Elephant's nose wasn't long, not one bit,
So he huffed and he puffed, then threw quite a fit.

One day in the jungle, while stomping around,
Elephant heard such a curious sound!
A rustle, a whisper, a chuckle, a snort,
And from the bushes, out came Tortoise, so short!

"Why are you grumbling, dear Elephant friend?"
Asked Tortoise with wisdom that never would bend.
"My nose is too short! It just won't extend,
I can't grab the leaves or even a bend!"

Tortoise thought long, then smiled so wide,
"There's a river that flows with magical tide.
Dip your nose in, but just beware—
For the river is tricky and doesn't play fair."

Elephant rushed to the river so fast,

PEPS PINNICLE

His stubby nose wiggled, he wanted to last.
With a splash and a splash, he dipped in his snout,
And then, oh dear, something stretched out!

His nose grew longer, longer, and long,
It stretched so far, it was surely wrong!
Elephant gasped, "Oh my, what is this?"
But he wiggled and jiggled and found it was bliss!

He could grab the bananas from trees oh so high,
He could swing it around, reach up to the sky.
He splashed in the river, oh what a delight,
With his long, stretchy trunk, he could play all night!

But soon Elephant noticed a curious thing—
His trunk wouldn't stop! It continued to swing.
It flopped in the bushes, it tangled in trees,
It got stuck in the branches, it buzzed with the bees!

"Help!" cried Elephant, "What shall I do?
My trunk's out of control! It's all gone askew!"
Then wise old Tortoise came back with a grin,
"Now that you've learned, let's pull it back in!"

So Tortoise and friends, with a pull and a yank,
Helped shorten the trunk, which had stretched like a plank.
It didn't go back to the stubby old thing,
But now it was useful, a marvellous swing!

Elephant smiled, his worries were done,
His trunk now perfect, just right for some fun.

And so in Congo Congo, when you see him today,
Elephant's trunk is here to stay!

So if you ever feel small, or not quite enough,
Remember, like Elephant, you too can be tough!
And though you might stretch, or stumble and fall,
You'll find what you need, and stand proud and tall!

Why Lion Roars So Loud

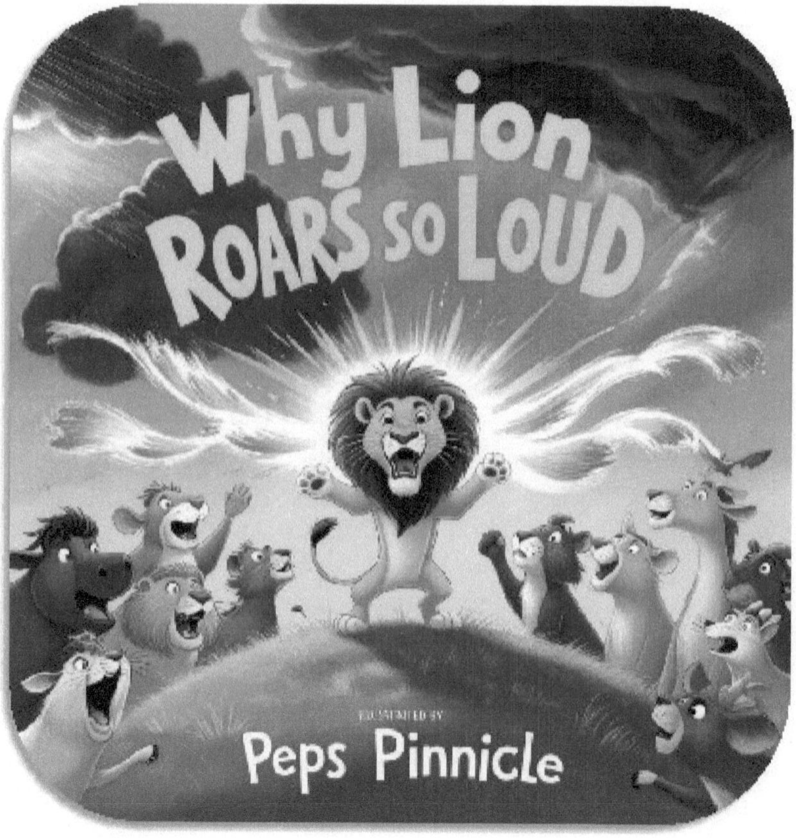

WHACKY AND WHIMSICAL POETRY

In Congo Congo, where the grasslands stretch far,
Lived a quiet young Lion who never did spar.
He'd slink through the bushes, paws soft on the ground,
But what made him different? He made not a sound!

The other animals giggled, "Lion, so shy!
Why don't you roar, why don't you try?"
But Lion just shrugged, with a gentle small grin,
"I'm happy in silence, it's peaceful within."

But deep in his heart, oh how he yearned,
To find his roar, for which he had learned,
All Lions had power, a voice of great might,
But for some reason, his stayed out of sight.

Then one day, as the sun blazed high,
A storm swept the plains, darkened the sky.
The winds howled fiercely, trees swayed and shook,
And all the animals ran for a nook.

The hyenas cackled, the monkeys screeched,
But Lion stayed still, just out of reach.
The sky split open with thunderous clap,
And suddenly Lion felt something snap.

From deep in his chest, a rumble arose,
It started to build from his tail to his nose.
He opened his mouth, unsure what would come,
And suddenly, oh! A roar had begun!

It burst from his throat, it shook the ground,

PEPS PINNICLE

A magnificent roar, a powerful sound!
The storm itself seemed to stagger and pause,
The animals stared, their paws without cause.

Lion roared louder, a thundering cry,
It echoed through valleys, it filled the sky.
The storm retreated, the clouds turned to flight,
Lion's roar had chased away the night!

When it was over, the jungle was still,
And Lion stood proudly, atop the high hill.
No longer quiet, no longer so small,
Lion had found his roar, and stood tall.

From that day onward, when danger is near,
Lion's mighty roar is what we all hear.
But he learned something too, after that wild chase—
A voice that's too loud can rattle a place!

So he roars when needed, when there's trouble to fight,
But keeps it in check when the days are just bright.
And now in the plains, when you hear that great sound,
Know that Lion has balance, his roar is profound!

How Chameleon Got His Colors

PEPS PINNICLE

In the land of Congo Congo, long ago,
Chameleon was plain, just one single glow.
He was green, always green, from morning to night,
And oh, how he longed for some color and light.

Zebra had stripes, so bold and so clear,
And Peacock's feathers would bring quite a cheer.
But poor Chameleon, with nothing but green,
Felt like the dullest creature ever seen.

He'd hide in the trees, try to blend in with style,
But deep down inside, he just longed to smile.
"Oh, why can't I shimmer, with purples and blues?
Why can't I sparkle, like the morning dew?"

One day, he sat by the watering hole,
When came along Tortoise, so wise and so old.
"You look quite glum, my dear colorless friend,
What troubles you so, that you can't seem to mend?"

Chameleon sighed, "I wish I could shine,
With colors so bright, so radiant, so fine!
But here I am, just this same old green,
The dullest creature that's ever been seen!"

Tortoise chuckled, and then gave a wink,
"Perhaps there's a secret, more than you think.
Go to the Rainbow, where the river does bend,
And dip in your tail—your troubles will end."

Chameleon raced to the rainbow so wide,

WHACKY AND WHIMSICAL POETRY

Its colors cascading down the mountainside.
He dipped in his tail, as Tortoise had said,
And suddenly felt a great tingle of red!

His body shimmered, then flashed into blue,
Then orange, then purple, then bright yellow too!
He could change on a whim, with a flick and a twist,
Now he had colors no creature could miss!

He danced through the trees, showing off his new glow,
"I can be anything, now don't you know!"
But soon Chameleon began to feel strange,
His constant shifting was hard to arrange.

"Too many colors!" he cried with a shout,
He jumbled them up, trying to sort it all out.
He turned pink when he wanted to blend in with red,
And suddenly turned into purple instead!

At last he sat down, with a worried long sigh,
How could he balance all these colors so high?
Then came wise Tortoise, with his slow little crawl,
"Remember, Chameleon, you can't have it all!"

"Your colors are gifts, but don't go too wild,
Find harmony in them, be free and be mild.
Use them with care, like a brush on a page,
And you'll shine like a star for every age!"

Chameleon nodded, and tried once again,
He learned how to shift, how to sparkle, and then—

PEPS PINNICLE

He found his true rhythm, his colors just right,
He'd glow when he wanted, or blend out of sight.

Now Chameleon's magic is known far and wide,
For he carries the colors of the rainbow inside.
And when you see him, in the jungle today,
He'll shimmer and shift in the most wondrous way!

WHACKY AND WHIMSICAL POETRY

PEPS PINNICLE

About The Author

Peps Pinnicle is a whimsical wordsmith and a passionate storyteller, whose imagination knows no bounds. Drawing inspiration from the enchanting world around him, Peps crafts delightful poetry that dances off the page, captivating readers of all ages. With a knack for blending humour and heart, he invites you into the vibrant realms of his mind, where the absurd and the beautiful coexist in perfect harmony. When he's not penning his latest verses, you can find Peps exploring nature, seeking out the extraordinary in the everyday, or sharing his love for storytelling with children. Join him on this whimsical journey through "Whacky and Whimsical Poetry," where each poem unfolds a new adventure, bringing laughter and joy to readers everywhere!

9 798822 703109